PICTURE-WORK

This edition published by Lector House in 2024

ISBN: 978-93-6138-016-7

Lector House LLP
Registered Office: H. No. 96, Block C, Tomar Colony,
Burari, Delhi – 110084, India
info@lectorhouse.com
www.lectorhouse.com

PICTURE-WORK

WALTER LOWRIE HERVEY

2024

LECTOR HOUSE LLP

PICTURE-WORK

BY

WALTER L. HERVEY, PH.D.

Contents

I.

The Problem and One of Its Solutions.

A friend of the writer, who has since attained to the dignity of a teacher of teachers, relates to the honor of his wise mother that when he was a boy she did not make him promise not to smoke or chew or play cards—probably compassing these ends in other ways—but she did exert her influence to lead him not to read Sunday-school books. For this warning, he says, he has never ceased to be thankful. In these days of supervising committees and selected lists, when standard literature, undiluted, has found its way into the Sunday-school library, such a course would not be warranted. But there are still thoughtful persons who do not feel that in the matter of Sunday-schools they are out of the woods yet.

"Do you know anything about Sunday-schools?" was asked of one of these, a representative woman.

"I'm sorry to say that I do," was the reply.

And there are other signs that the number is increasing of those who believe that in the choice of a Sunday-school the greatest care must be exercised. Some there are, who, it may be through over-conscientiousness, are fain to give up the search in despair, preferring to teach their children at home.

There is probably no other Sunday-school that, in point of order, quiet seclusion of classes, professional preparation of (paid) teachers, can compare with the "Religious School" of Temple Emanuel in New York City. But there is no intrinsic reason why the mechanical and pedagogical difficulties might not one day be as successfully removed everywhere as in this model school; and why they may not be removed in every grade.

In the infant classes, through the beneficent influence of the kindergarten, there are already signs of promise. In the senior departments the problem is less complicated. But in the classes where is found "the restless, wide-awake, active, intense, ingenious, irrepressible boy," or "the girl who is just beyond girlhood and yet can scarcely be regarded as a woman," and her awkward, self-conscious, misunderstood brother—here the problem remains, and no one denies that it is a hard one. Who cannot at this moment see with his mind's eye a picture of such a class—on the one side a vision of inattention, insubordination, irreverence, on the other, incompetence, blindly, consecratedly, painfully doing his—or her—best?

In all things relating to the common schools there is a quickening of popular interest and of professional spirit. The time is at hand when none but trained experts will be allowed to teach. Is the instruction and guidance of young minds in matters pertaining to the Heavenly Father and the things of the unseen world a task less difficult, delicate, important, than the teaching of arithmetic and geography? The question answers itself. It follows that the religious and moral instruction of our children will one day be put on a firmer and more scientific basis.

In this reform there are three steps: the securing of proper external conditions for thought and feeling—in blunter words, the banishment of hubbub; the systematic training of the teacher; the enrichment of the lesson by giving to it reality, meaning, and life. The last of these ends is the only one here under consideration. To this end there are doubtless several ways. "Picture-work" is one of these, and, it is believed, one of high importance. That it is neglected is beyond question. To point out its value and set forth its method are the aims of this little book.

II.

Types of Picture-Work.

In the Dresden Gallery, the writer once saw two children, brother and sister, one ten and the other twelve, looking at the Sistine Madonna. They entered the room, and without heeding the crowd there gathered, almost instantly fixed their gaze upon the picture. For many minutes they seemed to be under a spell. They were drinking in something. The great picture was speaking to them—to their very souls. And they understood something of its message. At all events they felt its influence—which is much better than merely to understand.

More striking, because more unexpected, was the influence of a large copy of the same picture upon a little boy not two years and a half old. Although this child was passionately fond of pictures, no other picture ever seemed to appeal to him as this one did. As soon as it was brought into the house he instantly began to examine it, and pass judgment upon it. He at once found the center of interest, the young child and his mother, then pointed to the angels, the "grandfather," and lastly to the "lady," but returned always to the "dear little baby Jesus." From this time the story of the birth of Jesus was the one story most loved by the child. And a collection of thirty or more madonnas ("mother-pictures," the child called them) by other great masters was a never-failing source of delight to him.

Even very young children appreciate the best pictures and the best stories. In fact the younger they are the better sometimes seems to be their taste. Are we doing all that we may to gratify, and at the same time to form, this taste?

But our term, "picture-work," includes more than pictures painted with the brush. Literature is full of pictures no less beautiful in theme and in execution, and even more important in meaning, than Raphael's masterpiece. The story of the good bishop, Monseigneur Bienvenu, as it is told for us in "Les Miserables," is a picture, and so are all such stories. Literature is full of them. The Bible is a treasure-house of masterpieces. More wonderful, too, are these story pictures, just as they are, if told so that they can be seen and felt, than they could ever be made with brush or pencil.

How may we gain the power to paint these pictures, helping when help is needed, standing aside when our bungling efforts would only destroy the interest and the charm—rub off, as it were, the delicate bloom?

To give help in finding the answer to these questions is the object of the chapters that follow. Meanwhile we return to our present theme. What is picture-work?

There is the main story and the telling of it—a work of art as we shall see—and there are also the side-lights, without which no story-teller can capture and hold his audience.

The story to be told, let us say, is the healing of the paralytic. But before the story begins, the ground must be cleared. The oriental house and bed must be pictured. Get a real specimen of each, if you can, of course.[1] Provide yourself with pictures in any case, but first of all, make an eastern house and bed yourself. A square paper box—a hat box will do—with a hole cut in the top, ready to be torn up when the time comes; a stairway made of paper, leading up the outside of the house to the roof; a small piece of felt—an old bed-quilt will serve equally well—with strings tied in each end, for the bed, to show how a bed could be let down, rolled, and "taken up"; with these accessories the teacher is ready to begin the work of sketching the real picture, the story of the miracle.

Not merely for children, but for grown folk too is this kind of picture-work a means of teaching. In a densely populated quarter of New York City there is to-day a minister who is not content with mere word-pictures. He brings into the pulpit the objects themselves—it may be a candle, a plumb line, a live frog, an air pump. With him the method is a success, as it has been with others. Does this seem crude? So are the mental processes of every forty-nine out of fifty the world over.

[1] See Chapter VIII., last heading.

Dr. Parkhurst in the second of those memorable sermons with which he opened the public campaign against Tammany, carried into the pulpit and showed his congregation the very bundle of indictments with which he was to strike the first blow for civic purity.

Ezekiel went still further, and not only used objects but actions to enforce and illustrate his terrible sermon:

"To the amazement of the people, setting them all awondering what he could mean, he appears one day before them with fire, a pair of scales, a knife, and a barber's razor. These were the heads, and doom was the burden of his sermon. Sweeping off, what an easterner considers it a shame to lose, his beard, and the hair also from his head, this bald and beardless man divides them into three parts; weighing them in the balance. One third he burns in the fire; one third he smites with the knife; and the remaining third he tosses in the air, scattering it on the winds of heaven." Thus the prophet under divine direction foretells the disgrace, division, destruction, dispersion of his people.

Not less striking is the story of Jeremiah's dramatic sermon as graphically told by Dr. Guthrie, from whom the preceding account has been quoted:

"The preacher appears—nor book, nor speech in hand, but an earthen vessel. He addresses his hearers. Pointing across the valley to Jerusalem, with busy thousands in its streets, its massive towers and noble temple glorious and beautiful beneath a southern sky, he says, speaking as an ambassador of God, 'I will make this city desolate and an hissing' . . . pauses—raises his arm—holds up the potter's vessel, dashes it on the ground; and planting his foot on its shivered fragments, he adds, 'Thus saith the Lord of Hosts, even so will I break this people, and this city as one breaketh a potter's vessel.'"

It may have been the inspiration of such examples as these that moved Beecher when, in the stirring days before the war upon the platform of Plymouth Church, after taking up one argument after another against abolition and answering it, he carried each one to the side of the platform and threw it over into the pile with its predecessors, saying, "That disposes of you." And in his famous Liverpool address, did he not, when speaking of the freeing of the slaves, throw down and trample upon actual chains?

At the heart of even the boldest of such instances of picture-work, there lies a true and universal principle. And we may be sure that we are more likely to err on the side of stiffness and conventionality (which is often sheer laziness and ignorance), than on the side of reality and life.

The unaided imagination—the power of the eyes to "see pictures while they're shut"—will, however, often serve us more safely, and not less surely. That was a vivid and memorable action-picture, drawn for us by Bishop Vincent, at a vesper service at the close of a Chautauqua Sabbath, in the "Hall in the Grove." "What if the Master himself were again on the earth at this hour, here at Chautauqua, and should come up the hill, through the trees yonder, and should stand between these pillars and speak to us now. . . ." The picture was complete and irresistible. We all saw and realized all that we needed to see and feel, in order to receive the lesson that followed.

But the imagination must be strengthened and fed by plenty of sense material. It can be trusted to respond with its pictures, provided it has been given material enough and provided these materials are skilfully brought to mind. In the following extract from the wonderful "Story of Jesus,"[2] which should be in the hands of every parent and teacher, we find a type of picture-work which illustrates this point, for it quickens and makes many calls upon the imagination: "Imagine traveling through a state no larger than Vermont, and finding not only apples and pears, quinces and plums, waving corn-fields, maples and cedars, but orange-trees fragrant with snowy blossoms, and heavy with golden fruit in January; figs and dates, pomegranates and bananas—all within a day's journey! The fields over which you pass glow like gorgeous Persian carpets. . . ." This is a part of the author's picture of Palestine.

And here is a bit of Archdeacon Farrar's graphic word-picture of Nazareth, where Jesus spent nearly thirty years of his life on the earth:

> "Gradually the valley opens into a little, natural-looking amphitheater of hills, supposed by some to be the crater of an extinct volcano; and then, clinging to hollows of a hill, which rises to the height of some five hundred feet above it, lie, like 'a handful of pearls in a goblet of emerald,' the flat roofs and narrow streets of a little eastern town. There is . . . a clear, abundant fountain, houses built of white stone, and gardens scattered among them, umbrageous with figs and olives, and rich with the white and scarlet blossoms of orange

[2] See Chapter VIII.

> and pomegranates. In spring, at least, everything about the place looks indescribably bright and soft; doves murmur in the trees; the hoopoe flits about in ceaseless activity; the bright blue roller-bird, the commonest and loveliest bird in Palestine, flashes like a living sapphire over fields which are enameled with innumerable flowers."

Who having once read, seen, and felt this picture can ever forget it or fail to feel the atmosphere of this place? It is thus we come to realize that Jesus Christ was really once a boy, a young man, a human being, on the earth. Even here, however, all possible helps in the form of pictures, maps, etc., must be called in as aids to the picturing power of the mind.

The number of "likes" in the two foregoing selections (there are at least eight of them expressed or implied) suggests the remark of a humble woman regarding the parables, "I like best the likes of Scripture." This word lies at the root of all picture-work. Whether in the parables of Jesus, who was the prince of teachers, or in the discourses of great preachers whose sermons teem with "likes," or in the story-teller's skilful comparison of place with place, people with people—Palestine with Vermont as to size, with England, Scotland, and Wales as to its divisions—Galilee, Samaria, and Judæa being "united because they had one government, one ruler; separate because of their peculiar characteristics, their definite boundaries, and jealous claims to special privileges"—in all the notion of likeness is the central point of the thought.

We never can know anything without having something to know it with. A "like" is the key that enables us to unlock and to enter the door of the unknown.

It is through picture-work also—to go a step further—that we come to have revealed to us our own characters. This type of picture-work is at once the most difficult and the most important of all. An example of such picture-making is chosen from an account written by Miss Wiltse, setting forth her method of making stories in order to suit the needs of specific cases among her pupils. Not every one has the love or the genius of Miss Wiltse, and no one can hope to win such success as hers at once; but it may be that by catching some of her spirit, studying her plan, and patiently practicing, we may learn this royal way of reaching the hearts of our children.

"There was in my kindergarten," she writes, "a little boy whose deceit and cruelty were quite abnormal; he would smile in my face with seraphic sweetness while his heavy shoe would be crushing his neighbor's toes. . . . He seemed incorrigible. At last I wrote a story entitled 'The Fairy True Child,' into which I put my strongest effort to reach this untruthful child. I told it to the class, and before it was concluded this boy's head was low upon his breast, his cheeks aflame with conscious guilt. No direct reference was made to him; no other child thought of him in connection with the story. The next day he asked to have it repeated, and his conduct was noticeably better; the story became his moral tonic, and one glad day he threw his arms about me, saying he wanted to keep his Fairy True Child always.

"Another child who was feeble-minded was helped to be free from his mental inertia and day-dreaming by a story written expressly for him, in which 'I AM THAT WHICH WILLS' was pictured as a fairy, coming softly to the little boy whose power to try was lost, kissing his eyes, breathing softly upon his lips, putting her finger softly upon his ears—making each more ready and attentive—and finally enthroning the little boy's own fairy in its place in his brain, where the fairy grows more and more princely, and the little boy more and more manly, trying hard, so very hard, to keep the dear little fairy on his throne."

Here, then, we have some of the types of picture-work: the picture and the story, the parable in its various forms, and the word-picture—whether of things or actions; illustrations or side-lights, the "likes" with which a skilful teacher illumines his teaching, and the objects, models, maps, and sketches on pad or blackboard, with which he re-enforces the lagging imaginations of his hearers.

What, then, is a picture? A picture is anything that helps us to see more clearly, feel more heartily, and act upon more faithfully the truth which is not or cannot be immediately present to our senses. The truth to be pictured may be the truth of people, places, and actions—external things; it may be the truth of character and of inner life—the things that are unseen, which we could never see at all except by the aid of real things or pictures of real things; just as, for example, our idea of God is built out of our experience of mountains, flowers, thunder-storms, our mother's tenderness, and our father's strength. These pictures may be drawn or painted; they may be expressed in words or in deeds, with pen or brush, with actions, with things.

Where to find our materials and how to use these tools with economy and effectiveness are the questions that next claim our attention.

III.

A Picture-Book, and How to Use It.

The Bible is a picture-book. It is history, literature, logic, philosophy; but, more than all these, for children and all who have the heart of childhood, it is a store-house of pictures.

The first thing needful for a teacher, if he would touch his pupils, is to see these pictures himself. This, we must admit, is seldom done. For it is one of the sad things about the human mind that it possesses the power to read the words that set the picture forth without seeing the picture, and without being touched by the emotion which only the picture can arouse. We can seem to pray the Lord's Prayer, for example, while in reality we are merely making articulate—sometimes inarticulate—sounds.

"I believe it would startle and move any one," said Robert Louis Stevenson, referring to the gospel of St. Matthew, "if he could make a certain effort of imagination and read it freshly like a book, not droningly and dully like a portion of the Bible."

Who of us has not been thus startled and moved? It may have been on hearing a story read by one who read as though he had seen the men and the events face to face. It may have been by being helped to realize and see by pictures or by being ourselves on the ground made sacred by the story, or, perchance, by being in the same case as those described. It may have been on reading the old stories "freshly, like a book," perhaps after many years, when the old-time droning and the dulness are forgotten, and the simple beauty and power of the old stories come home to us. At such times we say, This is the very Word of God. Were ever pictures painted like these?

Thomas Hardy says of one of his characters that, like every healthy youth, he had an aversion to the reading of the Bible. Some of us know what that means, though we did not know it was *healthy*. Better, we might almost say, that the child spent his time in some other way than to read the Bible or be taught it, only to conceive a dislike for its stories. Better a child never went to Sunday-school than that he should go to have interest deadened. He may wait many a year before the freshness returns.

"Two grand qualifications are equally necessary in the education of children," said Horace Mann, "love and knowledge." The teacher of the Bible must indeed *know*—not know about, merely, but be personally acquainted with—the old patriarchs, their dress, occupation, country, way of life, and character; the judges, likewise, the prophets and kings, the children of Israel as a people, the apostles and their friends, and, above all, Christ himself. Does it make little difference whether we think of Christ as an oriental or as an Italian; whether as clad in the turban and flowing white robes of the East or in more conventionalized attire; whether as he is pictured for us in the vivid and startling colors of the artist Tissot, or in the cold conventional steel of our grandmother's best parlor; or the base woodcuts of some modern lesson leaves?

To us as well as to our Lord himself it makes a vital difference whether his youth was spent amid arid wastes—as many of us picture Palestine—or in the peaceful beauty of such a retreat as that described for us in Archdeacon Farrar's picture.

We must indeed have knowledge, as full, as exact, as personal as it can be made for us or as we can make it for ourselves. And from this will come *love*. The more full, exact, and personal our vision, the more deep-seated will be our love. We should therefore seek our knowledge at first hand. We should look upon "helps" as we regard crutches—good until we can walk alone; bad the instant they keep us from using our own powers, seeing with our own eyes.

In picture-work, as in everything else, love is the principal thing. A teacher of little children, whose privilege it is to help them to enter into loving appreciation of buds and leaves, soil and roots, winter and how everything prepares for it, spring and how it wakes everything to new life, must herself love nature. No "science" falsely so called will suffice. "*Do you really love nature?*" as President G. Stanley Hall has said with an indescribable emphasis on every word, is the question of questions to ask such a teacher. "*Do you really love the pictures of the Bible?*" is likewise the question of questions for the parent and teacher whose high privilege it is to lead children from the first of their acquaintance to love the great Picture-Book.

IV.

Side-Lights.

"Can you apply a parable?" says one of Robert Louis Stevenson's characters. "It is not the same thing as a reason, but usually vastly more convincing."

The spiritual truth which we would have enter the child's mind—how is it to gain admittance? Not by a surgical operation; much less by the use of a foreign language or—what is quite the same thing—of abstract language. Not by any direct means, but indirectly, by objects, scaffolding, types, the story, and the illustration.

"Every natural fact is a symbol of some spiritual fact, and no spiritual fact can be understood except by first knowing the natural fact, which is, as it were, its double." It is so with the child, it is no less true of grown folk. If it were not for the world of nature—of boundless horizon, ceaselessly flowing rivers, of deaths and resurrections, of parasites—we should be powerless to grasp the truths of the world of spirit. The circle in the water, for example, the apples on the plate, one specked, then all rotten, these all are but letters of the alphabet by which we spell out *Influence*.

There must first be in the thing-world—to give one more example—the "rolling-stone," "the last straw," "the bird in the hand," "the leaven," the ore, worth seventy-five cents as ore, worth four dollars as bar-iron, worth $400,000 when worked up into hair-spring, before we can understand, or explain, or talk about the corresponding things in the realm of the unseen. Which is only another way of saying that he whose mind is not filled with the truths of nature is but ill furnished for understanding the truth of God.

How may we gain this power to enrich our teaching with side-lights?

1. By studying the great masters of the art of illustration. Beecher, Spurgeon, Dr. Parkhurst, are all worthy of emulation. Beecher testifies that in his early preaching the power to illustrate was only latent. He found that he was not reaching his hearers and he began to search for "likes." He went about his farm, upon the streets, among mechanics, in fact everywhere, with the thought of the next Sunday's sermon in his mind, saying, "What is this like? what will that illustrate?" A glance at his sermons shows them full of side-lights from business, life at sea, from the farm and the home, from mechanical processes, as the cutting and polishing of precious stones, and very often from nature.

In a recent sermon Dr. Parkhurst illustrated his single point from botany, physics, physiology, a ship, and from the actual experience of two men engaged in a life-and-death struggle with the same appetite.

But the power of these great preachers is only the reflex of the method of Christ himself. No man had greater power in picture-work. In range, fertility, aptness, and result, the word-pictures of Jesus stand alone in the history of teaching, just as in respect of beauty and power they stand alone in literature.

2. The power of picturesque speech is acquired through earnestness and love of truth, as well as through rich experience of nature and of common life. This is hinted at by Emerson: "A man's power to think and to speak depends on the simplicity of his character, that is, upon his love of truth. . . . Picturesque language means that he who employs it is a man in alliance with truth and God. A man conversing in earnest, if he watch his intellectual processes, will find that a picture arises in his mind, contemporaneous with every thought, which furnishes the vestment of the thought. Hence good writings and brilliant discourse are perpetual allegories. This imagery is spontaneous, provided one have lived sufficiently to fill his mind with the raw materials of such pictures. One bred in the woods shall not lose his lesson in the roar of cities. . . . At the call of a noble sentiment, again the woods wave, the pines murmur, the river rolls and shines, and the cattle low upon the mountains, as he saw and heard them in his infancy. And with these forms, the spells of persuasion, the keys of power are put into his hands." And as it is with contact with nature, so it is with first hand experience of life in any form.

3. Practice. The effects of practice have already been cited in the case of Beecher. It is one of the mournful facts of human life that so many powers that might have been brought out by practice always remain in the latent state. Practice story-telling, practice finding "likes," and you will find before long that there is growing up in you a new power, just as if you were to discover in your organism a stop, by pulling which you could jump ten feet in the air. "Practice is nine tenths. A course of mobs is good practice for orators. All the great speakers were bad speakers at first." And a course of nephews and nieces is the best of practice for story-tellers, and for those who would be adepts in the use of side-lights.

A word of caution. Great care must be used not to make the stories and illustrations more prominent than the truth we wish to illustrate. Dr. William M. Taylor tells of a conversation with a carpenter in which he advised him to use certain decorations. "That," said the carpenter, "would violate the first rule of architecture. We must never construct ornament but only ornament construction." So it is in story-telling. Never tell a story for its own sake, merely, but for the sake of the truth that lies embedded in it. A story or an illustration must grow as naturally out of the subject as a flower grows out of a plant.

V.

Stories and Story-Telling.

That was a profound and true saying uttered by President G. Stanley Hall not long ago, that "of all the things that a teacher should know how to do the most important, without any exception, is to be able to tell a story." And a student pursuing a university course in education, after seeking to know what stories to choose, where to find them, how and to whom and wherefore to tell them, touched the same truth when he said, "It gradually dawned upon me that if I knew how to tell a story, I had mastered the main part of the art of teaching." For to know a good story is to have literary and pedagogic taste; to adapt or make a good story for children is both to know the secret of the mind of a child and to have creative power; to tell a good story is to be a master of a noble art.

The child's thirst for stories—has it no significance, and does it not lay a duty upon us? And yet the insatiableness of the child's thirst is often paralleled by the inadequacy of the teacher's power to satisfy it, and by the parent's despair at being so bankrupt of material.

In his admirable suggestions for making the Sunday-school able to appeal to the interest and the respect of boys and girls who are no longer children, and whom to treat as children is an offense against good taste and Christian charity, Bishop Vincent recommends, among other things, "lectures and outlines, and independent statements by individual pupils and teachers." Story-telling, both by teachers and pupils, is here suggested as a means of further enrichment.

The "wholes" of Scripture narrative, whole books, whole lives, whole stories *told as wholes* by the teacher or by a single pupil, and not picked out piecemeal by the teacher from halting individuals—these are the things that in the class give interest and that in the mind live and grow and bear fruit. "Moral power is the effect of large unbroken masses of thought; in these alone can a strong interest be developed," and from these alone can a steady will spring.

He who has never read or heard as a whole, at one, or at most, two sittings, the story of an entire book of the Bible, as Jonah, Daniel, Job, or one of the Gospels, has missed one of the chief sources of interest and power.

Our course through the Bible—incident by incident, verse by verse, here a little, there a little, years of "lessons," but no idea even of the life of Christ as a whole—is not unlike the toilsome road traversed by the boy "reading" Cæsar as his first Latin author: so many separate, mutually repellant parts, but no wholes, no idea of what it is all about; or it may be compared to the route of the milk-man—a stop at every other house, and never a good run.

Not one of these plodders, the Sunday-school pupil, the young Latin student, the milk-man's hack, can be looked upon as a model of spiritedness or of continuity.

A teacher of English in the old days, when literature was used chiefly as a clothes-line on which to air grammatical linen, was once guilty of giving out a lesson in Washington Irving—so many constructions, figures, analyses, so many pages, and no more. The end came in the *middle* of the ride of the headless horseman. But by the time the next class studied Irving the teacher had met with a change. The limit of the first lesson was set according to the structure of the story. The pupils were told to read the story.

"Only read it!" said they. "Aren't we to do anything with it?"

"No," said the teacher, "you are to read it *for fun*."

Should one be in danger of being misunderstood in saying that we do not have enough of reading the Bible for fun, for the pure enjoyment of its stories and of its matchless pictures? The rest will come in due course. It will come just so surely as the story is *realized.*

But important as reading is, telling is incomparably better. The eye of the teacher is then fixed on the class, not on the book; the tone is conversational, the hand is free to gesture and to draw. One can grasp the whole of the story and the whole of the situation. One can bring out dramatic power. For there are few stories that do not have some dramatic quality, both in the making and in the telling. The following points kept in mind will aid the teacher:

1. The story must have a beginning, concrete, interest-compelling, curiosity-piquing. "All things have two handles; beware of the wrong one."

2. It must have a climax, properly led up to, easily led down from; and that never missed.

3. Many good stories have rhythm, recurrence, repetition of the *leit motiv*. "The Three Bears" is a favorite for this reason, among others. The commands of the Lord to Moses were regularly repeated thrice in the Bible story; in the book of Daniel the sonorous catalogue of flute, harp, sackbut, and the rest, comes in none too often for the purposes of the story-teller.

4. All good stories have unity; parts well subordinated; the main lesson unmistakably clear; the point, whether tactfully hidden or brought out by skilful questions, never missed.

This use of stories by exactly reproducing them is naturally the teacher's first method. There follow naturally the *adaptation* of stories and the making of *original* stories. The latter way must be dismissed with a single word of caution. Beware of a certain fatal facility in reeling off "made-up" stories. Have you not heard such teachers and such stories? The latter at least are not true, or healthy, or wholesome. They are about unreal people who do unnatural things. They are a poor, ragged device for covering the nakedness of barefaced moralizing.

No one who has tried to tell Bible stories to children, whether young or old, can fail to appreciate the need of adaptation: of enrichment and expansion on the one hand, of condensation on the other. Suppose the story to be told is the parable of the Good Samaritan. There must first be preliminary work. The minds of the children must be made ready, not merely for the lesson, as, for example, by a talk on the meaning of "neighbor," but also for the story. This latter kind of preparation for three reasons:

1. To give your hearers something of the same knowledge about the road from Jerusalem to Jericho, the relations of Jews and Samaritans, the standing and dignity of high priests and Levites possessed by those who heard the parable from the lips of Jesus.

2. To give the setting of the story—time, place, people, customs, atmosphere.

3. To make the language, the steps, the moral, as intelligible to your hearers as they were to the young lawyer to whom the story was first told.

The need of the first way of filling in the picture is brought out by Mrs. Gaskoin in the "Children's Treasury of Bible Stories," Part III.:

> "Pages might be written about this parable, for every line is full of teaching, wrapped in beautiful words. But my object just now is only to draw your attention to the circumstance that the third person who passed the wounded man—and the only one who cared about his sufferings and took pains to relieve them—was a Samaritan. On this the point of the story turns. First a priest, and then a Levite, whose very offices alone should have made them ready helpers, had shunned their poor countryman, and had passed on without even a word of sympathy. But the person who did pity him, and, indeed, showered kindnesses upon him, was, not only neither priest nor Levite, not only a mere stranger—but a Samaritan. Now to say this was the same thing to the "lawyer" who was listening to the tale as to say that he was an enemy. The Lord could have chosen no stronger expression; in using it he spoke quite as plainly as when, once before, his words had been these: 'I say unto you which hear: Love your enemies, do good to them which hate you, bless them that curse you!' Clearly, then, it is only by understanding how the Jews felt toward the Samaritans, that we can grasp what the blessed Savior meant when he said that every disciple of his must love his 'neighbor' as himself."

A striking example of the mode of using a full knowledge of customs and people to enrich the story is given by the same author in the following vivid word-picture of the thrilling experience of Zacharias. After describing the method of choosing by lot the priests to take charge of the temple services, the narrative continues:

> "To Zacharias, however, one autumn, the coveted lot did fall, and leaving his quiet home, he went up to Jerusalem, and there entered at once upon his sacred duties. They lasted

for eight days, including two Sabbaths. . . . Every morning at nine o'clock, and every afternoon at three, a priest entered the Holy Place to sprinkle the incense-offering on the golden altar. He was accompanied by an assistant priest, who withdrew as soon as he had made the necessary preparations. The privilege of sprinkling the incense-offering, like the other priestly functions, was bestowed by lot. One day, during his week of attendance in the Temple, the lot fell upon Zacharias. So, in his white robes, with bare feet and covered head, he went slowly up, through court after court, to the entrance of the Holy Place. Then a bell rang, all the other ministrants on duty in the Temple took their places, and the people assembled in the various courts composed themselves for prayer. Zacharias disappeared within the sacred enclosure, and in due course his attendant left him alone there, separated from the Holy of Holies itself only by the splendid Veil-of-Partition. Silvery clouds of fragrant smoke presently arose from the kindled incense—then, kneeling before the altar, he paused, in prayer and adoration. Suddenly he became aware that he was not alone. Lifting his eyes he saw, to the right of the altar, a glorious angel, who thus addressed him, dispelling his gathering fear: 'Fear not, Zacharias, for thy prayer is heard, and thy wife Elizabeth shall bear thee a son, and thou shalt call his name John.' . . . 'Whereby shall I know this?' he asked, hesitatingly. And the angel, answering, said unto him, 'I am Gabriel, that stand in the presence of God, and am sent to speak unto thee, and to show thee these glad tidings. And behold thou shalt be dumb and not able to speak, until the day that these things shall be performed, because thou believest not my words, which shall be fulfilled in their season.'

"Meanwhile the people were anxiously waiting for Zacharias to return. His reappearance would be the signal for the laying of the sacrifice upon the altar, accompanied by a joyous outburst of the beautiful Temple music. Great, then, was their uneasy wonder at the unusual delay. But at last he did appear."

An illustration of what is meant by re-telling the old story in a modern way for modern hearers is found in the following characteristic extract from a sermon of Dr. Parkhurst's on the text, "And he arose and came to his father":

> "The prodigal had not enjoyed nearly as much as he expected—what he had arranged to enjoy. His scheme had collapsed; his experiment broken down. Going away from home and living as though he had no home had not worked as he expected that it was going to. Lonely, ragged, hungry, he thought the thing all over and said to himself: 'I think I had better go home.' He had let go of home, but home had declined to let go of him. He had been his father's boy for twenty years or more, and his experience in the far country had not been quite able to cure him of it. Home still had a pull upon him."

While many of the stories both of the Old and of the New Testament need expansion rather than contraction—think of trying to bring the masterly story of Jonah or the wonderfully simple tale of the Shunemite's son into any smaller compass!—yet the need of condensing the long stories, of Abraham, Joseph, David, Daniel, for instance, is obvious, for we must give the children a picture of the whole life and character of these great and simple figures. To this end selection and suppression are necessary.

The various books mentioned in a later chapter are all more or less successful in the attempt to recast the old original story. So perfect is the original form, however, that the task is one of extreme difficulty. Yet it must be attempted by every teacher, and it is certainly worth a trial. The following suggestions may prove helpful in both modes of adaptation:

1. Use direct discourse. It will require an effort to keep yourself (in your embarrassment) from taking refuge behind the indirect form, saying, for example, "And when he came to himself he said *that he would* arise and go to *his* father and tell him *that he had* sinned."

2. Choose actions rather than descriptions, the dynamics rather than the statics of your subject. Those of us who have grown away from childhood tend to reverse the true order, to place the emphasis on the question, "What kind of a man was he," and not on, "What did he do." Let what he did tell what he was. Your story will thus have "go," as all Bible stories have.

3. Use concrete terms, not abstract; tell what was done, not how somebody felt or thought when something was being done; be objective, not subjective.

4. A story-teller should, in short, have taste. To form this taste it is indispensable that he should not read, but *drink in* the great masters: Homer, Chaucer, Bunyan, Hawthorne ("The Wonder Book," for example), and above all the Bible itself. No one can absorb these without unconsciously forming a pure, simple style and getting a more childlike point of view and way of speech. Modern writers and modern ways of thinking are, in general, too reflective, self-conscious, subjective, and, where children are concerned, too direct, bare, "preachy."

5. But the secret of story-telling lies not in following rules, not in analyzing processes, not even in imitating good models, though these are all necessary, but first of all in being *full*—full of the story, the picture, the children; and then, in being morally and spiritually up to concert pitch, which is the true source of power in anything. From these comes spontaneity; what is within must come out; the story tells itself; and of your fulness the children all receive.

Finally, the points of practical story-telling may be thus outlined:

1. See it. If you are to make me see it you must see it yourself.

2. Feel it. If it is to touch your class it must first have touched you.

3. Shorten it. It is probably too long. Brevity is the soul of story-telling.

4. Expand it. It is probably meager in necessary background, in details.

5. Master it. Practice. Repetition is the mother of stories well told; readiness, the secret of classes well held.

6. Repeat it. Don't be afraid of re-telling a good story. The younger the children are, the better they like old friends. But every one loves a "twice-told tale."

VI.

Some First Principles: Unity, Reality, Order.

Unity.

One of the greatest of American preachers never goes beyond "firstly." He makes but one point in each sermon. But he makes that point, drives it home, burns it in, wears a crease in the brain that nothing can ever iron out. Every picture—and those sermons are full of pictures—bears upon that one point, and every argument and lesson, for which the pictures have been laying the foundation, is a part of the same unity. You never hear him say, "And we learn further," but always, "The same truth comes out in another way." One is never more than two bases away from the home plate. It is not a cross-country run, but a game of score and tally.

At the opposite pole from this intensive method is the typical Sunday-school lesson. The typical Sunday-school lesson is—is it not?—hodge-podge. Does the last lesson always bear upon the lesson of to-day? Is to-day's aim single? Do you hold before your mind the one point, the one picture, that your pupils shall carry away with them as an everlasting possession, or do you have in mind to display so many pictures, so many points, that some must needs take effect?

It is easier—at least it is lazier—to provide *many things* than to prepare *much*. One can rake over an acre more easily than dig one post-hole. And the deeper you go the harder grows the digging. But it's the last six inches of hole that makes firm the top two feet of post.

Now pictures help toward unity of aim in a lesson in two ways: they help to elaborate the one main point—twenty illustrations of one point, not twenty points from one illustration; they help to teach us the law of unity, for a true picture has but one theme, is always simple.

Reality.

"The great trouble with the stuff taught in our schools is that so much of it always remains *stuff*, and never gets worked up into *boy*." So said Dr. Parkhurst, in a sermon from the text, "Taste and see that the Lord is good." The only way to work up the raw materials of a boy into real boy is to bring him into touch with them, to have him taste, see, handle. But in order to be tasted these materials must be real. And to make them real is the first duty of the teacher. It is also his hardest task. For consider what it costs to make a thing so real to yourself that it can't help being real to some one else! Ah! there's the rub. It costs to do that—costs time, pains, life.

How long did the Lord make Ezekiel lie on his left side, and how long on his right side, without the relief of turning over from one side to the other, before he judged him ready to deliver his message with a due sense of the reality of its import? Three hundred and ninety days "for the iniquity of the house of Israel," forty days more "for the iniquity of the house of Judah"; each day for a year. After that there was no lack of a "realizing sense" in Ezekiel. He had "been there" himself. And was it by way of mere luxury or was it from pedagogical necessity that the Lord showed himself last of all to Paul also, and sent him into the desert, for a year or more, to think it over and get a real grip on the experience? It was a true instinct that made Thomas, the doubting one, want to reinforce a sight-picture by a touch-picture. A dose of the same "doubt" would be a tonic to much of the pale "faith" in the world.

When I was a boy I wrote, after the fashion of the day, an "essay" on a subject about which I had the slenderest knowledge. A tannery lay on my way to school, and the tanner would have been friendly and communicative, but the encyclopedia article, "Leather," was my sole authority. You may imagine the result: a cold, dead thing, not in the least savoring of real leather. On the other hand, when I became a man, I traveled a thousand miles merely to see, and hear the voice of, a master whom I admired and whose picture I wished to have hanging in my mind. Who has not, when freed from the dead atmosphere of the schools, done a like thing? And with what gain to the precious sense of reality!

The whole country, not long since, was touched—many people were shocked—by the news that a Christian minister had dared to see with his own eyes the evils he was fighting, the existence of which he had been challenged to prove. Many good people at that time thought he had made a mistake. He said, "It is necessary that some one see these things. Do you think that I would be so base as to ask another to do what I would not do myself?" The result has proved the soundness of this position. No one now doubts that Dr. Parkhurst was in the right. For not only were the facts shown to exist as alleged, but (and this is the point) the man himself who had seen them was so filled with a burning sense of their terrible reality, that he clung to his point with an everlasting grip, carried it triumphantly, and laid the foundations of our "civic renaissance."

The vast audience who heard Bishop Thoburn, missionary to India for thirty years, at Chautauqua, was stirred to its depths by the simple power of the man. What was the secret of his power? It did not lie in his bodily presence; it grew out of what the man had done. He was a man of action. He had given his life, and had lived. His speech was of that which he had lived. You felt that he had a right to speak—for every sentence had behind it weeks of real life.

Who has not felt the same when listening to one who speaks of that which he does know? And who has not felt the difference when trying to listen to one who talks, but whose words are not loaded with life?

You must have seen, acted, felt, if you would make your hearers see and feel and act. Talk is cheap, especially borrowed talk. It is not the story in the lesson quarterly that you can build into the lives of your class; it is the story in you. It is the picture that has become a part of your life, that will be most likely to be built into the fabric of theirs.

Order.

The way in which a subject lies in the mind of an ordinary, unregenerate adult, one may be safe in saying, is just the wrong way—the way in which it should not be presented to a child. The order of exposition is in general the reverse of the order of acquisition. The natural man who has forgotten how things look to the eyes of a child has a tendency to put things wrong end to; word first, thing last; precept first, example last; to plunge *in medias res* without introduction—in short, to put the mental or spiritual cart before the horse. And it requires self-sacrifice to reverse the order, enter into the limitations of a little child's mind, see with his eyes, think his thoughts.

It is a favorite simile among writers on education that the mind is not unlike a field, and that the steps of instruction answer to the successive stages of the farmer's work. First there is the preparation of the soil, then come the planting, the cultivating, and in due time the harvest, the mill, and the market. Two of these steps, the preparing and the applying, concern us here; the work of presenting and elaborating is a theme by itself, and has been treated in a separate chapter.

1. Preparing the ground: Approach.

The art of "getting a good ready" is an art worth mastering. In sermon or Sunday-school lesson alike the beginning is the main concern. It is a good plan to seem to waste time at the start. Nine tenths plowing, harrowing, marking out, one tenth sowing, and (as we shall see) no looking for a crop at all, is a just proportion for the most of our lessons. We shall be always safe in counting upon a sufficient number of stony-ground hearers to justify us in clearing the ground, and making it mellow with interest and expectation. And even those who would receive the word with gladness cannot take it in unless they have something to grasp it with, cannot hear without something to hear with. And this must be given them by the teacher.

We are here at the very heart of the science of teaching. A little two-year-old child will serve us as an example. He is to be put in bed in a strange room, and is to go to sleep alone. Spring the idea upon him and he will reject it. Prepare him for it, by telling him a story of a little boy who went to bed in a new room, a new bed, and all alone, and he is eager for the hour of bed-time. When the time comes, the picture already in his mind, of a little boy, a new room, a peaceful going to bed, welcomes the actual experience, point for point. The wise mother has made a nest for the experience.

So might a teacher prepare the minds of his pupils to receive the idea of ninety millions of miles.

"If any one there in the sun fired off a cannon straight at you, what should you do?"

"Get out of the way," would be the answer.

"No need of that," the teacher might reply. "You may quietly go to sleep in your room, and get up again; you may learn a trade, and grow as old as I am—then only will the cannon-ball be getting near, then you may jump to one side! See, so great as that is the sun's distance!"

So writes a German teacher—explaining the law of apperception, of making a nest for the idea.

We cannot understand—cannot even see or hear—the absolutely new. Every new plan or way of looking at things, or doctrine, is received into the mind on one condition only—that it be introduced by a comrade already there. Then when the new idea calls from without, its fellow answers from within, and an entrance is effected.

The bearing of this upon our theme is illustrated by the plan of a school principal, recently described to me, to eradicate the plague of stealing that had broken out in the school. He talked to the pupils of giants, drew out the children's ideas, and by effective picture-work made the creatures out to be an ugly, uncanny crew. He then was ready to declare to the children that he had discovered a giant in the school, and in due time told them his name—Selfishness, I think it was—and then described his evil works. The moral of this story is that the plan worked, and stealing disappeared from the school from that day.

Who of us teachers might not be emulous of becoming thus skilful in mellowing the soil and making it warm in the genial sunshine of true picture-work?

2. Gathering the crop: Taste.

If deliberation is a virtue at the start, brevity and patience are a necessity at the finish. When the teacher has planted an interest-awakening picture in the minds of the children, his main work is done. He may safely leave them to make the application. He has supplied the cause; the effect will take care of itself. It is often convenient and suggestive to remember that children are not fools. "A child knows a thing or two," 'tis said, "before he knows much of anything." And one of the very first things he knows is how to put his finger on the moral in a story; and he can feel it long before he knows it. But that is when he is left to himself. If you take the helm, ten to one he'll know without feeling, which is the curse of us all. Better, if we must choose, that he feel without knowing in terms, than indulge in mere intellectual casuistry.

In your childish haste to have a crop or to see what was going on under ground, did you ever unearth the newly-planted row of peas? And was that row ever so green and straight and thick-standing as those that had been let alone? But the plants of love to God and moral taste are tenderer than these. They must be shined upon, warmed, and watered many days before they are ready to give an account of themselves. Love is a silent thing before it is outspoken. True feeling has few words, is not self-conscious, likes not to be asked questions. In its own good time it wells up and finds vent in deeds, and even in words.

The deepest thing a teacher does is to form taste. But all taste grows slowly, by unconscious accretion. The Chinese money-changer sets his apprentice at work handling good money only. For ten Years he touches nothing else. He can then detect a counterfeit coin. How? Perhaps he cannot tell how. His way is surer, deeper. He feels it. He has taste. So with the building of the taste for good books, for pictures, for nature. It is a slow process—many a book to be absorbed, picture seen and loved, and mountain and flower and sunset gazed upon, before taste is formed.

And the taste for godliness, for religion, is no exception. It is the finest and rarest of all tastes, and hence is the slowest and quietest of all in its development.

But did you ever see, in the hot house, shall we say, of the Sunday-school, seed sown, harvest reaped, yes, and cakes taken from the oven, within the limits of a single half hour? Does the figure halt, or was it a miraculous quickening of the processes of nature, or was it in truth a great mistake and a sin against natural spiritual growth?

There need be no fear, then, that the children will not feel, and in time know, the meaning, for them, of their stories and pictures. And a wise teacher well knows the ways of helping them: by questioning, *not* directly, and by hiding the moral so near the surface that it will come forth of itself.

VII.

How to Learn How.

The foregoing chapters have dealt chiefly with the theory of picture-work, answering the questions what and why. But practical teachers will go a step further and ask where to find and how to use materials, what to do first, what next, in becoming expert in using and making pictures, stories, and illustrations; in short, how to learn how. Those who are not of the practical sort should omit this chapter, and no one should expect to enjoy or profit by it who has not the time and the will to go through the exercises described.

Models. A study of some of the remarkable pictures of secular literature will reveal many points in story-telling.

Mark how Chaucer made such a picture of his Canterbury pilgrims that not only the color, the action, and the characters of the scene, but also the very atmosphere of the jolly crowd has been clear and vivid for more than four centuries.

Macaulay boasted that he would write a history which would supersede the latest novel on the tables of the young ladies of the day. How did he accomplish this? Read his "History of England" and learn the secret of the power to picture.

Study George Eliot's "Silas Marner" to learn how to tell a story. The interest never flags, the proper perspective is always maintained, light and shade are in due proportion, and the lesson to be learned is taken, not as a bitter dose, but as one drinks in the fresh air of a clear May morning.

Study pictures of Bible scenes by great masters to see what aspect of the scene—what moment of the event—the painter chose as the climax of interest and meaning. Although the aim in Sunday-school work is spiritual and not artistic, the heart will be reached more surely if the eyes are appealed to and a subordinate artistic aim is kept always in mind.

What is the favorite view-point in picturing Noah's ark (the procession—a source of never-failing interest to old and young—is a conspicuous feature); in Abraham's sacririfice (Andrea del Sarto seizes the moment when Abraham is about to slay Isaac and the ram appears in the thicket); in the early life of Moses? Note also the subjects in the life of Christ oftenest chosen by the artist.

In what parables does Christ choose a definite locality well known to his hearers, definite characters, a definite point and only one, a definite purpose, and a clearly defined and applied moral? In the presentation of which parables do we *not* find simple language, direct discourse, a dramatic style, and a question in order to drive home the point?

Try the effect of substituting in any one of the parables indirect discourse for direct, statements for questions.

Make a study of the Sermon on the Mount with a view of finding opportunities for picture-work.

On how many and on what occasions did Jesus use objects in his teaching? Might he not have gotten along without using the objects themselves on those occasions? What seems to have been his purpose? What was the result?

Seeing. Suppose that you were an artist searching in the Bible for scenes to paint:

1. What picture would you find in Matthew VIII., verse 1? verse 2? verse 3? verse 4? Can you see (and hear) each of these?

2. What is *the* picture in the whole passage (verses 1-4)? How many elements has it, in respect of number, form, color, sound, atmosphere?

3. Which of these should be chosen in telling the story to children, and in what order?

4. How many pictures are there in verses 5-13? What is the central picture?

5. In verses 23-27. How many pictures are there in this passage? Which is the central picture? How would you lead the pupils to see it? What first? what next? what last?

6. In Matthew, chapters ix. and xiii. How many separate pictures are there? Which are the most important to try to see? What objects, pictures, drawings, maps, would you use in making it real to your class?

Construction. In the previous chapter there was brought out the need of adapting the stories of the Bible to the comprehension of modern hearers. Suggestions were given both for cutting down and filling in.

Choose a story, as of the brave Hebrew boys who stood by what they thought was right even in captivity; the young king who asked God to give him wisdom and whose way of ruling showed that his request had been granted; the shepherd boy whom the Lord chose; or choose an incident, or a period of a year of the life of Christ (as the "Year of Beginnings," the "Year of Popularity," the "Year of Opposition").

Subdivide each of these into smaller stories or incidents (Daniel, for instance, had three great tests, each complete in itself, and lived under three kings), then combine into a whole, applying the principles of story-telling and of adaptation.

Test your story by telling it to a child or a group of children. Tell the same story not once but many times.

Choice. Do not pad. Avoid diffuseness. Put in only those details that are salient—that leap out at you—that are necessary to the picture and the meaning. Any one can put in everything. It is only the born story-teller, or the one who will sit down by the side of a child and patiently observe the points that the child sees and likes to hear, that can be trusted to put in and to leave out just the right points.

Try writing out the story of Jonah, without the book. Compare your work with the original. How might you have been less diffuse? What necessary points did you omit? Did you use more or fewer general terms than the original? Were your words and expressions so picturesque as those in the text?

Examples. By way of illustrating the meaning of the foregoing points, it may be interesting to note the difference in concreteness, *i.e.*, in the *picture*, to be found in the following paragraphs, all of which are intended to mean practically the same thing.

(*a*) One bidden to obey and refusing, but afterward obeying, is a better example of obedience than one who obeys in word but not in deed.

(*b*) Some one who was requested to do something refused in word, but obeyed in deed; another complied, but only in word. Which was the better example of obedience?

(*c*) If some one in authority should tell some one to do something and he should refuse but afterward comply, and should tell another to do something and he should say that he would without doing so, which of these really would perform the will of the one who gave the command?

(*d*) A certain man had some children. One day he told one of them to go and do some work that he wanted him to do. But the child said that he wouldn't, etc.

(*e*) Compare with these the same thought clothed in the concrete and picturesque words of our Lord himself:

"But what think ye? A certain man had two sons; and he came to the first, and said, Son, go work to-day in my vineyard.

"He answered and said, I will not: but afterwards he repented, and went.

"And he came to the second, and said likewise. And he answered and said, I go, sir: and went not.

"Whether of them twain did the will of his father?"

It would be equally possible to take the same clear-cut, dramatic picture and load it down—smother it—with words. But this kind of picture-work it is unnecessary to illustrate.

Expression. Read each of the parables of Jesus, picturing in your mind everything that can be seen, heard, or felt. "Put yourself in his place" regarding every one spoken of. When you have thus pictured the story, and while you are picturing it, read aloud, or tell the story. The expression will take care of itself—*if only you see and hear*. In this simple principle is contained the whole art of expression, *i.e.*, of giving forth something which is within.

Environment. What kind of country was Palestine? If Palestine were taken up from the shore of the Mediterranean and planted on your state, where would Dan and Beersheba lie respectively? Wherein did its divisions differ, in respect of people, surface, products, occupations?

The four routes of Christ's principal journeys are given as follows: Bethlehem to Jerusalem, 6 miles north; Bethlehem to Egypt, 250 miles southwest; Nazareth to Jericho, 60 miles southeast; Nazareth to Jerusalem, 65 miles south. Trace these routes on a sand map and on the blackboard. Describe the country passed through, the occupations of the people, the mode of travel, the length of time required.

Account for the roughness of the road from Jerusalem to Jericho.

What kind of place was Cæsarea Philippi, and what kind of stream is the Jordan at that point?

Sketching. The teacher should practice until he can make, with the flat crayon, something that looks like a mountain, a road, a tree—a scumble for the foliage and a stroke or two for the trunk, a man—two strokes will do for him (some teachers prefer to cut out pictures and pin them on the board). It must be admitted that this method of trial and error is dangerous. But there are self-taught teachers who do pretty well.

Map-drawing. To learn to sketch a map is a more hopeful task. Every one should be able to follow on pad or blackboard a campaign, a flight into Egypt, and a march up into Canaan; and to trace the journeys of Jesus and of Paul.

The following directions will be found helpful in drawing, free-hand and with only two construction lines, the map of Palestine:

Draw a horizontal line, and on it with the span of the hand, or with any convenient unit, measure three units, indicating their extremities by the figures 1, 2, 3, 4, from left to right. At the right extremity of this line, which we designate 4, draw a vertical line five units in length (4-9). From the upper extremity of this line draw to the left a line parallel to 1-4, one unit in length (9-10). Join points 1 and 10 with an irregular line, thus indicating the coast. A perpendicular let fall from 10 to 3 would indicate the course of the Jordan, the source lying nearly opposite 8, the Sea of Galilee opposite 7, the Dead Sea between 4 and 5; and Judæa, Samaria, Galilee, and Phœnicia will each occupy, roughly speaking, one and a half units. The principal mountains, cities, routes, may be indicated by initials, signs, or in any other appropriate ways. Each unit being 40 miles in length, the dimensions of Palestine and its parts may be derived. This same system may, of course, be used in drawing any map.

Miss Lucy Wheelock says that "the most satisfactory map is one which the teacher makes herself, drawing the outlines with a blue marking crayon on a sheet of white silesia, or finished cotton cloth, and putting in thin strips of wood or rollers at top and bottom, so that it will hang easily."

The sand table, especially with work for younger children, is indispensable. This every one can learn to make and manage and can fit out with the needed materials. Let no one shrink from the simple task of getting together the equipment and learning to model a map of Palestine.

The following description of the way of making a sand map of Palestine has been kindly furnished by Miss Juliet E. Dimock of Elizabeth, N.J., whose theory and practice in primary classes are alike admirable:

"Any carpenter will make for you a board, four feet six inches long, and two feet six inches wide, with a raised edge of one and one half inches. Paint the surface a bright blue, to represent the waters of the Mediterranean. Procure about fifty pounds of molders' sand from a stove foundry. The new sand is preferable to that which has been used for casting, owing to its lighter color. Study a good map of Palestine until you have a clear idea of the coast-line, the sea-coast plain, the mountain region, with its principal peaks, the Jordan valley, and the eastern table land."

(A relief map is desirable as a guide. The relative heights of mountains are given in Hurlbut's "Bible Geography." A cross-section of Palestine showing relief is given in the "Bible Study Union Lessons," Old Testament History, Progressive Grade, First Quarter, Appendix pp. (V.), (VI.). The Bible Study Publishing Co., 21 Bromfield Street, Boston, Mass.)

"Cut a paper pattern of the rivers and have them cut out of tin by a tinsmith. Use mirrors for the waters of Merom, the Dead Sea, and the Sea of Galilee, and white cord for the roads.

"When you are ready to go to work, place the board on a table and empty upon it your box of sand, which should be dampened until it can easily be molded by the hand. Raise the head of the board, until the children can see your work; if the sand is damp enough to keep its place, it can be inclined at an angle of forty-five degrees. At first the children will be interested in seeing you form the map; the coast-line, with its "camel's hump" for Mt. Carmel, the mountains, with snow-capped Hermon towering above them all, the seas, rivers, roads, and finally the white paper boats on the Mediterranean.

"Take five minutes every Sunday for a supplemental lesson on the history of the land, beginning with the first settlement of the country by the Canaanites, the family of Noah's grandson. Use the map also, whenever it is possible, to illustrate the lesson for the day; either as a map, or by building up the sand into a city, a garden, a temple, or a palace. The supplemental course might begin with the Garden of Eden, with as great a variety of trees, flowers, and animals, as may be easily obtained. And by turning the board around, the map of the ancient world may be made, and the stories of Noah, Babel, and Abram's journey from Ur of the Chaldees. Use small objects to make the places on the map, and replace them with initial blocks when the children are sufficiently familiar with the story to tell it to you. A very little ingenuity on the part of the teacher will suggest the objects to be used, which can be readily cut out of colored card-board.

"After school, return the sand to its box and pour at least a quart of water over it. It will then be in good condition for next Sunday's use."

Specifics. True picture-work has, as we have seen, a true bearing upon the question, How to help children conquer their faults. "Don't," even "Please don't," is ineffectual and unpedagogical. So is every means that is direct and negative instead of indirect and constructive. It is a thousand times easier to empty a tumbler of air by filling it with water than by the use of the air pump.

And so, just as we know that singing has a marvelous power to sweeten and calm the spirit of a young child, so a story is often the shortest and the most effective means to bring him to himself. A story is a specific. The right story will heal its proper disorder. There is danger here, 'tis true; "the intent to teach," as Herbart writes, spoils it all. Stories should be given as food rather than as medicine. There is all the greater need, therefore, for practice.

Find, adapt, make up stories to meet the needs of a child who is idle; of one who is mean, lacks self-control, is slovenly, careless, untruthful, etc.

Texts. On the other hand, it is just as necessary that illustrations attach themselves to their proper principles, as that principles find the concrete key that will serve as their open sesame into the child's mind.

Mr. Barrie tells of a newspaper writer who never conversed five minutes with a friend without getting a suggestion for a leader or a "story." The teacher ought to be no less fertile in finding texts, and in pressing everything he meets—whether in books, in newspapers, or on the street—into the service of the Sunday-school lesson.

For example, the street car on which you ride to school or to business in the morning suddenly stops. It stands still three, five, fifteen minutes. You are late. Twenty others are late. Reason, a careless truck-driver has driven an inch too near the track. What does this illustrate?

A pound of cotton, worth a few cents, may be made into yarn and become worth more; into chintz and be worth still more, etc. What is the truth hidden in this fact?

A thoughtful teacher, in reply to the question, "What stories have you found especially helpful?" contained in the blank on story-telling (Chapter X.), gave the following:

"Cato's words, 'Carthage must be destroyed' (the power of words); Hercules at the parting of the ways (the necessity of choice); Macbeth's 'I have lived long enough' (the end of a wasted life); The Ancient Mariner—'He prayeth best' (the secret of prayer); the parable of the wicked husbandmen (irreverence)."

VIII.

Books, Pictures, and Illustrative Material.

The teacher should be a capitalist. He should not run dry every Sunday, and fill in during the week only enough for the next lesson; as a schoolboy who fills his mind with facts and empties it on examination day. The true teacher is independent of the "Quarterly." He uses it but does not lean on it. For the facts there given are, as a rule, isolated, and so half dead; the illustrations are at best warmed over. Neither can give a strong head of steam. There is not enough, and what there is is cold.

Other remedies for this condition are suggested elsewhere. Here it is urged that the teacher must be a reader of books. The following are given as types. They have been selected after searching the lists of many publishers, and are recommended only after a personal examination:

Books Telling the Story of the Bible.

There are many Bible stories for children, some of them good, but most of them far from ideal when both the story and the pictures are considered. Those with highly colored, gaudy pictures should be shunned as they tend to give low ideals morally and spiritually as well as to corrupt the child's artistic taste. To publish a story of the Bible with illustrations taken only from great masters is a good work waiting for some one who wishes to be of service to the world.

"The Story of the Bible from Genesis to Revelation," by Charles Foster. Charles Foster Publishing Co., Philadelphia, Pa. 75 cents.

Of the many Bible stories published this is the most complete and the most popular. In the matter of pictures, however, it is poor.

"Children's Treasury of Bible Stories," by Mrs. Herman Gaskoin. Macmillan & Co. Three parts, 18mo, 30 cents each.

The best Bible story we have found. It is most suggestive and interesting, showing how to picture Bible scenes.

"Stories from the Bible," Rev. Alfred J. Church. Macmillan & Co. 256 pp., $1.25.

Excellent as giving a condensed account of the Bible narrative in Bible language. The teacher who uses these stories will often find it necessary to supplement them with suitable introductions and side-lights.

"The Sweet Story of Old," by Mrs. Haskell. Dutton. 4to, 50 cents.

A small book of Bible stories for young children, with pictures which are quite good.

"First Steps for Little Feet," by Charles Foster. Charles Foster Publishing Co. 50 cents.

Bible stories told in simple language for the youngest children. Fair outline pictures.

"The Story of Jesus," by Louisa T. Craigin. Illustrated with one hundred full-page illustrations from the designs of Alexander Bida, together with many other pictures of the Holy Land. Fords, Howard & Hulbert. $10.00.

A beautiful and sympathetic account of the life of Jesus, especially rich in descriptions of Palestine and in other materials for word-pictures. The numerous pictures of landscapes and scenes from the life of Christ are helpful.

The same in paper covers in 15 numbers, 50 cents each.

"From Olivet to Patmos." The First Christian Century in Picture and Story. By Louisa Seymour Houghton. American Tract Society. $1.50.

"The Life of Christ in Picture and Story," by Louisa Seymour Houghton. American Tract Society. $1.25.

The last two books contain some poorly executed but well-chosen pictures of Bible lands, showing architecture, costumes, street scenes, etc.

Books About Palestine.

"The Land and the Book," by W. M. Thomson. Harper & Bros. $8.00, $6.00.

Recommended by a high authority as the best book on Palestine for a teacher who can own only one.

"Boy Travelers in Egypt and the Holy Land," by T. W. Knox. Harper & Bros. $3.00.

"Sinai and Palestine in Connection with their History," by Dean Stanley. A. C. Armstrong. $2.50.

An excellent standard work.

"Pictured Palestine," by James Neill. Anson D. Randolph. $2.25.

Shows the contrast between eastern life and our own. Very good pictures illustrating many phases of oriental life.

"In Scripture Lands." Scribner's. $3.50.

Beautiful pictures.

"Earthly Foot-Prints of the Man of Galilee," by Bishop John H. Vincent, D.D., LL.D., Jas. W. Lee, D.D., Robert E. M. Bain. New York and St. Louis: N. D. Thompson Publishing Co. $4.75.

Four hundred fine, large photographic views and descriptions of places connected with the earthly life of our Lord and his apostles.

Books on the Use of Stories and Illustrations.

"The Use of Stories in the Kindergarten," by Anna Buckland. Ginn & Co. 15 cents.

"The Place of the Story in Early Education," by Sara E. Wiltse. Ginn & Co. 132 pp., 50 cents.

Two suggestive and helpful essays that every teacher should read.

"Yale Lectures on Preaching," by Henry Ward Beecher. Fords, Howard & Hulbert. $2.00.

An inspiring book. The chapter on "Rhetorical Illustrations" is especially applicable, but the entire work, although written for preachers, has rich stores of instruction and guidance for teachers.

"The Art of Illustration," by C. H. Spurgeon. Wilbur B. Ketchum. $1.25.

A book by a master giving the secret of his art.

Stories and Themes.

"Parables from Nature," by Margaret Gatty. Macmillan & Co. 2 vols., 18mo, $1.50.

A wonderful book, in which nature is used to typify spiritual truths. It should be owned by every mother and teacher.

"Parables. Laws of Nature and Life, or Science applied to Character," by Louisa Parsons Hopkins. Lee & Shepard. 15 cents.

Brief and suggestive.

"Stories of the Saints," by Mrs. C. Van D. Chenoweth. Houghton, Mifflin & Co. $1.00.

Supplies a want which should be more "felt" than it is. Is it not as important that our children should know the story of Christian saints and martyrs as that of Greek gods and heroes?

"Kindergarten Stories and Morning Talks," by Sara E. Wiltse. Ginn & Co. 212 pp., 75 cents.

"Stories for Kindergartens and Primary Schools," by Sara E. Wiltse. Ginn & Co. 50 cents.

"A Brave Baby and Other Stories," by Sara E. Wiltse. Ginn & Co. 50 cents.

These three books are storehouses of inspiration and models of story-telling.

"Child Stories from the Masters," by Maude Menefee. Kindergarten Literature Co., Chicago. $1.00.

An excellent selection of themes from poets, dramatists, and the Bible. The teacher will do well to study the originals and try to improve upon the stories given.

"Child's Christ-Tales," by Andrea Hofer. Woman's Temple, Chicago. $1.00.

Choice illustrations from the masters. Suggestive tales and parables.

"The Kindergarten Sunday-School," by Frederika Beard. Kindergarten Publishing Co., Woman's Temple, Chicago.

An attempt to solve the infant class problem. Three series of lessons, each having sequence and unity. Suggestive in its plan, and likely to help teachers to improve upon the models given.

Books to be Read for the Sake of a Better Understanding of Child Nature.

"Study of Child Nature," by Elizabeth Harrison. Chicago Kindergarten Training School. $1.00.

"Children's Rights," by Kate Douglas Wiggin. Houghton, Mifflin & Co. $1.00.

"A Boy's Town," by W. D. Howells. Harper & Bros., New York. $1.25.

"Being a Boy," by Charles Dudley Warner. Houghton, Mifflin & Co. $1.25.

"The Story of a Bad Boy," by T. B. Aldrich. Houghton, Mifflin & Co. $1.25.

"The Mill on the Floss," by George Eliot. Harper & Bros. Popular ed. 75 cents.

"Cuore, An Italian Schoolboy's Journal," by Edmondo de Amicis. N.Y. Crowell. Illustrated edition. $1.50.

Pictures and Books from which Pictures may be Culled.

"The Life of Christ as Treated in Art," by F. W. Farrar, D.D., F.R.S. Macmillan & Co. $8.00, $5.00.

"The Christ Child in Art," by Henry Van Dyke. Harper & Bros. $4.00.

"Sacred and Legendary Art," by Mrs. Anna Jameson. Longmans, Green & Co. 2 vols., 16mo. $2.50.

"The History of Our Lord as Exemplified in Works of Art," by Mrs. Anna Jameson. Illustrated. 2 vols. Longmans, Green & Co. $8.00.

All the above are standard works and are excellent.

"The Earthly Footprints of Our Risen Lord," by Fleming H. Revell. 4to. $1.50.

A continuous narrative of the four gospels according to the revised version, illustrated by numerous half-tone pictures. The selection is not so choice as one could wish, yet many of the pictures are by the best artists, and present a consecutive pictorial story of the life of Christ.

"The Photographs of the Holy Land." Globe Bible Publishing Co., Philadelphia. $3.00. The same in cheaper style in eight portfolios at 10 cents apiece.

Photographs of classic and modern pictures of the child Jesus and of other Biblical subjects. Unmounted, card size, 3¾ cents each; cabinet size, 7½ cents each. A catalogue in German will be sent on application. R. Tamme, Dresden, Germany.

There is no duty on pictures.

Blue print copies of pictures of Biblical scenes by the old masters and by modern artists. Mr. Alfred A. Hart, 221 West 109th Street, New York City. Card size, one cent each.

Clear, durable, excellent; of a kind likely to develop good taste. The low price makes it possible to encourage children to make collections of their own. A single secular school has used over twelve thousand of these pictures.

The Christmas catalogues of publishers often contain serviceable pictures.

The standard histories of art are full of illustrative material. The teacher should be ever on the alert.

Objective Helps; Blackboard Sketches.

Cards for children to prick and sew. Bible Study Publishing Co., 21 Bromfield Street, Boston, Mass.

Scroll of history. See "The Modern Sunday School," p. 297. John H. Vincent.

Sunday-school Museum. Read description of one at Akron, in "The Modern Sunday School," p. 301.

Illustrative Blackboard Sketching, by W. Bertha Hintz. E. L. Kellogg & Co. 53 pp. 30 cents.

A helpful guide designed for those entirely ignorant of the art of drawing, who nevertheless like to work out their own way of putting a lesson, for the eye as well as for the ear, in preference to ready-made blackboard exercises and "pictured truth" at second hand.

IX.

False Picture-Work.

A book on helps, to be truly helpful, must deal with negative as well as with positive matters—those things which we ought to leave undone as well as those we ought to do. Any treatment of true picture-work is lacking in completeness, not to say in candor, which does not say a word about false picture-work.

If there were only some way of crawling into the inside of the children's brains, and marking the effect of the alliterations, juxtapositions, and symbolisms of what goes by the name of picture-work! Can't we devise a meter for estimating the precise emotional and spiritual value of a board filled with marks in various colors in the form of anchors, hearts, keys, crosses, not to mention other less sacred things?

I once saw a "chalk talk" given to two hundred Sunday-school children. *Dramatis personæ*: three parrots; one unrecognizable, it was so badly drawn; a second, indifferent; the third, capital, a speaking likeness. The last was perched on S. T. Moral: "Honesty is the best policy." The children were as delighted as if the text had been taken from the Bible and as interested in the display as if it had possessed the slightest value.

"But," it is urged, "the children are always interested in such things." Yes, and they would be more interested still if you showed them a monkey or displayed red, green, and blue lights. The law of interest tells us what shall *not* be placed before the children—"Nothing that is not interesting"—but as a guide to what we *shall* give them it tells but half the story. The other half is, "*Not everything that is interesting, and not anything just because it is interesting.*"

Let this caution not be misunderstood. The children must use their eyes. To expect children to follow your stories by ear, and make up their mind-pictures out of whole cloth or from the few objects and pictures that can be shown them, or to remember texts and lesson points out of hand, is to suppose them ready to graduate into the senior department. Let us have more blackboards. An individual board for every pupil, if possible, and the more use—wise use—of blackboards the better. But many "blackboardists" have yet to learn that it is possible to be apt without being alliterative, that one may be extravagant without being effective, sensational without being spiritual. In short, they seem not to understand that common sense applies even to blackboard work.

What are the points in good blackboard work? To be quite dogmatic, for the sake of brevity, good blackboard work is:

1. Simple. "Blackboard ingenuities, dissolving from acrostic into enigma, and from enigma into rhyme are not necessary" and they are harmful besides. They distract, distort, make dizzy. The best blackboard work has the fewest lines, the most unity in its variety, the least approach to anything like a maze.

2. Clear. The best blackboard work is that which is easiest to follow, hardest to forget.

3. Varied. Our stock symbols are worked to death. Is it *right* to use the cross as commonly as you would a letter of the alphabet? Find something new or give the blackboard a vacation. It is not necessary that there be a quarter hour on every day's program for blackboard work. Who has not spent a "bad quarter of an hour" when the "exercise" was perfunctory?

4. Descriptive. All maps and plans, sketches of roads and rooms, of mountains and rivers, are good, because they help us to form for ourselves the picture which we must see in order to grasp the meaning of the story. For example, we may illustrate the Mount of Transfiguration; first with four figures, then six, then four; the winding road to Emmaus, two figures—straight lines, merely—and a little farther on, a third; the upper room, its occupants represented by marks or initial letters. Anything is helpful that gives a notion of position, number, form, contrast, sequence, change.

5. Free, living, personal. The best blackboard work is that which is freest. Children are impressionists. For them the broad side of the crayon is

better than the point; two strokes better than twenty.

The best blackboard work is that which grows before the children's eyes, which is made, not unveiled. Two minutes of rough sketching in the lesson hour is better than two hours of patient putting in of finishing touches beforehand.

The best blackboard work is that which is original, personal. That which is given in the "lesson helps" is just what you should not use. It is not yours. If it does not help you to find your own way, it is useless—and worse than useless, because it tempts you to borrow without inspiring you to create.

6. In fine, the mission of the blackboard, as of all picture-work, is to help us to see the truth in the world or the truth in our own selves by showing us a truth that is easier to see or that is nearer at hand than that which we would learn.

Like all picture-work, it fulfills its mission when it serves as a scaffolding, when it is kept subordinate. It fails when it obscures the truth, not helps to build it. False picture-work is anything that stands in the way of our seeing truth; as when we cannot see the woods for the trees—cannot see the Sunday-school lesson for the bizarre exhibitions on the blackboard.

X.

A Coöperative Study.

In order to find out what Sunday-school teachers are doing in the matter of stories, illustrations, and picture-work generally, the writer prepared and distributed to a thousand teachers the following blank:

One response NOW is worth twenty a month hence.

STORY-TELLING.

To Sunday-school Teachers:

For the purpose of devising means for the better preparation of Sunday-school teachers, the President of the Teachers College, New York, requests the teachers in your Sunday-school to answer the following questions.

To save time and trouble use both sides of this sheet.

Whenever possible answer by crossing out the term that does not apply.

In every case where the answer is based on experience with children, state the age of the children.

Please do not hesitate to return this blank, even if you have answered but a few questions.

Sources.—To illustrate the lesson do you use Bible stories, stories from good literature, or stories invented by yourself?

Subject.—Do you find your children more interested in stories of people or of nature?

Kind.—Which of the stories have you found more effective, modern or classic? Stories told or read? True or fictitious? Those based on poetry or prose? Stories in which the moral is set forth or hidden?

Experience.—What stories are you going to use in the Sunday-school lesson for next Sunday?

Precept.—If you do not use stories, what other means do you employ to enforce religious and moral lessons? Do you "moralize," and if so, with what obvious result?

Environment.—What means do you use of making the dress, customs, etc., of Bible people seem real to children?

Picture-work.—Do you use blackboard illustrations? What other objective helps?

Examples.—What stories have you found especially helpful?

Purpose.—What is your purpose in using stories in the Sunday-school?

Principles.—Do you succeed in having such unity in the lesson that the stories all contribute to one main thought? Mention five requisites for a good story-teller.

Mention five qualities in a good story.

To these questions fifty-eight replies were received. Very few, however, gave the ages of the children, and the smallness of the number of replies—which after all is by no means discouraging—tends to vitiate the data as bases for generalization.

Space forbids giving more than a single group of typical answers. Some of the most helpful of the suggestions have been embodied in the foregoing. Further replies from thoughtful teachers will be welcome.

Question—Mention five requisites for a good story-teller.

Answers:

Sympathetic voice, manner, and face.

More knowledge of the subject than one wants to use.

The teacher must be interested, bright, imaginative, clear in thought and expression.

Clear apprehension of the point to be made, clear knowledge of the subject, understanding of the peculiarities of his hearers, tact in making application, and dramatic power.

Power in word-painting—with a sense of perspective.

Unconsciousness of self.

A gift for mimicry.

Graphic description.

Sympathy with children.

Power to hold attention and keep to the main thought.

Animation, personal magnetism, originality, wit.

Conciseness, force.

Pleasant manner.

Ability to repeat a story without hesitation.

Power to put one's self into the time, circumstances, etc., of the story.

Love of story-telling.

Quiet manners.

Gestures, good voice.

Small [easy?] words.

Ability to make the children help tell the story, by making them gesture, point, express sorrow, surprise, etc., and answer questions.

A good story-teller asks intensely interesting questions at exactly the right point.

A passage from Herbart forms a fitting close to this study:

"The intent to teach spoils children's books at once; it is forgotten that every one, the child included, selects what suits him from what he reads, and judges the writing as well as the writer after his own fashion. Show the bad to children plainly, but not as an object of desire, and they will recognize that it is bad. Interrupt a narrative with moral precepts, and they will find you a wearisome narrator. Relate only what is good, and they will feel it monotonous, and the mere charm of variety will make the bad welcome. Remember your own feelings on seeing a purely moral play. But give to them an interesting story, rich in incidents, relationships, characters, strictly in accordance with psychological truth, and not beyond the feelings and ideas of children; make no effort to depict the worst or the best, only let a faint, half-conscious moral tact secure that the interest of the action tends away from the bad toward the good, the just, the right; then you will see how the child's attention is fixed upon it, how it seeks to discover the truth and think over all sides of the matter, how the many-sided material calls forth a many-sided judgment, how the charm of change ends in preference for the best, so that the boy who perhaps feels himself a step or two higher in moral judgment than the hero or the author, will cling to his view with inner self-approbation, and so guard himself from a coarseness he already feels beneath him. The story must have one more characteristic, if its effect is to be lasting and emphatic; it must carry on its face the strongest and clearest stamp of human greatness. For a boy distinguishes the common and ordinary from the praiseworthy as well as we; he even has this distinction more at heart than we have, for he does not like to feel himself small, he wishes to be a man. The whole look of a well-trained boy is directed above himself, and when eight years old his entire line of vision extends beyond all histories of children. Present to the boy therefore such men as he himself would like to be."

Printed by Libri Plureos GmbH in Hamburg,
Germany